NIGHTMARE BUGS!

Giant Hissing COCKROACHES

T0191353

By Natalie Humphrey

Gareth Stevens PUBLISHING

HOT TOPICS

Please visit our website, www.garethstevens.com. For a free color catalog of all our high-quality books, call toll free 1-800-542-2595 or fax 1-877-542-2596.

Library of Congress Cataloging-in-Publication Data

Names: Humphrey, Natalie, author.
Title: Hissing cockroaches / Natalie Humphrey.
Description: Buffalo, NY : Gareth Stevens Publishing, [2025] | Series:
   Nightmare bugs! | Includes bibliographical references and index.
Identifiers: LCCN 2023042320 | ISBN 9781538292150 (library binding) | ISBN
   9781538292143 (paperback) | ISBN 9781538292167 (ebook)
Subjects: LCSH: Madagascar hissing cockroach–Juvenile literature.
Classification: LCC QL505.7.B4 H86 2025 | DDC 595.7/28–dc23/eng/20231208
LC record available at https://lccn.loc.gov/2023042320

First Edition

Published in 2025 by
Gareth Stevens Publishing
2544 Clinton St
Buffalo, NY 14224

Designer: Andrea Davison-Bartolotta
Editor: Natalie Humphrey

Photo credits: Cover, p. 9 Aastels/Shutterstock.com; series art (texture) Video_Stock _Production/Shutterstock.com; series art (lines) Hananta S/Shutterstock.com; series art (sign) Mr Doomits/Shutterstock.com; series art (trees) Wilqkuku/ Shutterstock.com; p. 5 Katrina Brown/Shutterstock.com; p. 7 7th Son Studio/ Shutterstock.com; p. 11 slowmotiongli/Shutterstock.com; p. 13 Artush/ Shutterstock.com; p. 15 Marco Rubino/Shutterstock.com; p. 17 Maximillian cabinet/ Shutterstock.com; p. 19 Vovalis/Shutterstock.com; p. 21 Guillermo Guerao Serra/ Shutterstock.com; p. 23 Emily Nestlerode/Shutterstock.com; p. 25 Kefca/ Shutterstock.com; p. 27 Aldona Gnas/Shutterstock.com; p. 29 ArliftAtoz2205/ Shutterstock.com; p. 30 Ilya Rudzis/Shutterstock.com.

Printed in the United States of America

Some of the images in this book illustrate individuals who are models. The depictions do not imply actual situations or events.

CPSIA compliance information: Batch #CS25GS: For further information contact Gareth Stevens, New York, New York at 1-800-542-2595.

Find us on

CONTENTS

Hissing COCKROACHES!

The Madagascar hissing cockroach is one of the biggest roaches in the world! This huge insect is so big, it looks like something you'd only find in your nightmares. But don't worry: The hissing cockroach can only be found in the wild on the island of Madagascar, a country along Africa's southeast coast.

Terrible Truths

An insect is a small animal with six legs. It has three main body parts: the head, **thorax**, and **abdomen**.

Hissing Cockroach BODIES

Hissing cockroaches are big bugs. They are between 2 and 4 inches (5 and 10 cm) long and can weigh up to nearly 1 ounce (28 g). They are usually dark black and brown in color. Unlike many other cockroaches, hissing cockroaches don't have wings.

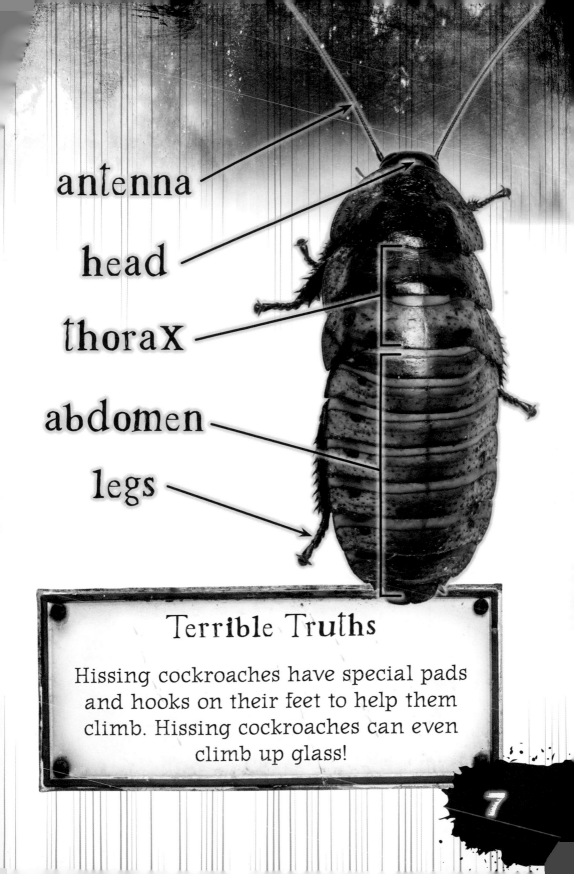

antenna

head

thorax

abdomen

legs

Terrible Truths

Hissing cockroaches have special pads and hooks on their feet to help them climb. Hissing cockroaches can even climb up glass!

A Loud HISS

Hissing cockroaches get their name from the way they keep their **territory** safe. When a hissing cockroach senses danger, it hisses to scare the other animal away. This hissing is loud and can make the cockroch seem bigger than it is.

Terrible Truths

Hissing is a sound that animals make that sounds like a long "s." A hissing cockroach's hiss can be as loud as a snake's or cat's hiss!

When a hissing cockroach hisses, it uses special holes on its back. These holes are called spiracles. They are usually used for breathing. The hissing cockroach pushes air out of its spiracles quickly. This makes a hiss sound.

Terrible Truths

Hissing cockroaches also hiss to **communicate** with other hissing cockroaches.

DETRITIVORES

Hissing cockroaches are detritivores. This means they eat dead things. Hissing cockroaches like to eat dead plants and animals. They eat food left behind by other animals too. Whether it's fresh or dead, a hissing cockroach will eat anything!

Terrible Truths

Hissing cockroaches usually eat plants more than any other food. They'll eat them dead or alive!

A detritivore's dinner is gross, but detritivores are an important part of their **ecosystem**. Detritivores like hissing cockroaches help get rid of dead things in their habitat, or the natural place where an animal lives. This helps keep it clean for all the animals living there!

Terrible Truths

By getting rid of dead things, detritivores also help to stop the spread of disease, or illness, in their habitat.

15

At HOME

Hissing cockroaches don't just eat dead plants, they live in them too! They make their home in dead leaves, logs, and other hiding spots. During the day, they hide out of sight. At night, these roaches come out to eat!

Terrible Truths

Hissing cockroaches don't like the light. If a hissing cockroach sees light, it will try to run away!

A Cockroach WITH HORNS!

Hissing cockroaches have a special plate above their head. On this plate, there are two large bumps that look like **horns.** These horns are called tubercles. Male hissing cockroaches use their tubercles to fight other males.

tubercles

Terrible Truths

Female hissing cockroaches
have tubercles as well, but
theirs are usually smaller.

Baby Hissing
COCKROACHES

When it's time to start a family, male hissing cockroaches hiss to draw in a female! The female keeps her eggs within her body. After 60 days, baby hissing cockroaches **hatch** inside the female's body and are pushed out. The baby roaches look like small adult roaches.

Terrible Truths

Baby hissing cockroaches are nightmare bugs on their own. These babies are white and almost clear when first born. They look like ghosts!

21

When a hissing cockroach grows, it molts! Molting is when an animal sheds its old, smaller exoskeleton. This allows a new exoskeleton to grow. Hissing cockroaches molt six times before they're fully grown.

Terrible Truths

An exoskeleton is the hard outer covering of an animal's body. Right after molting, a hissing cockroach is soft and white in color. Gross!

old eXoskeleton

23

A Cockroach COLONY

A group of hissing cockroaches is called a colony. One hissing cockroach colony will usually have one male in charge. The colony is also made up of many females and their babies. The male hissing cockroach keeps his colony safe from both other males and predators.

Terrible Truths

Female hissing cockroaches in a colony are social. This means the females seem to like being with other females and don't usually fight.

25

Stay AWAY!

Hissing cockroaches might look like a nightmare, but they aren't a nightmare for people! Hissing cockroaches aren't attracted, or drawn, to light. This means that even if a person's home is nearby, the hissing cockroach won't usually go inside. Hissing cockroaches don't often leave their territory.

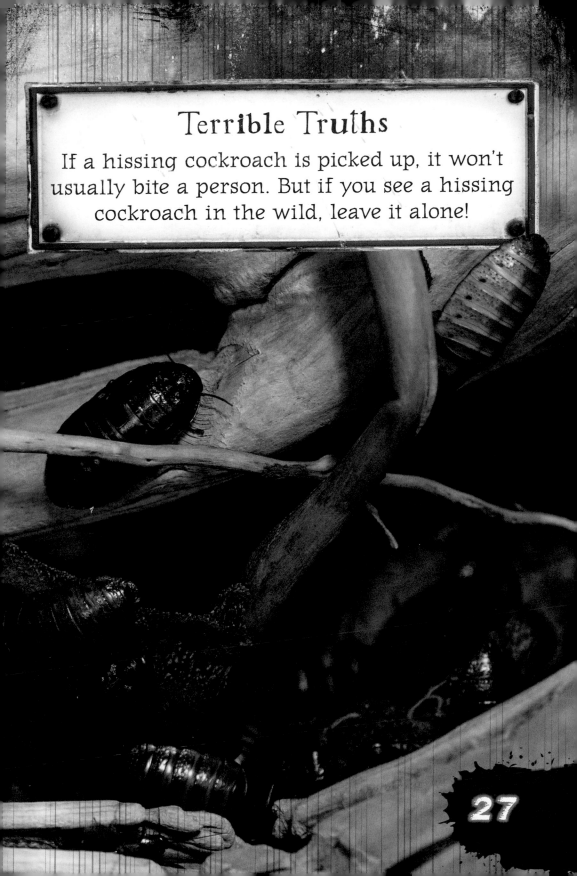

Terrible Truths

If a hissing cockroach is picked up, it won't usually bite a person. But if you see a hissing cockroach in the wild, leave it alone!

Pet Giant
COCKROACHES

Even though hissing cockroaches look a bit scary, some people keep them as pets. Hissing cockroaches don't need a lot of special care. Hissing cockroaches mainly just need a **tank** with enough spots for them to hide and food for them to eat.

Terrible Truths

Some people keep hissing cockroaches as food for other pets. Hissing cockroaches can be great dinners for lizards and snakes.

Tiny Terrors
GIANT HISSING COCKROACHES

Size: 2 to 4 inches (5 to 10 cm)

Appearance: dark brown and black

Life span: two to five years

Where Do They Live? Madagascar

Diet: dead plants and animals

Nightmare Fact: Hissing cockroaches will eat their exoskeleton after they shed it!

FOR MORE INFORMATION

BOOKS

Gitlin, Marty. *Hissing Cockroaches.* Chicago, IL: World Books, 2020.

McAneney, Caitie. *This Book Hisses!* Buffalo, NY: Gareth Stevens Publishing, 2020.

WEBSITES

Maryland Zoo: Madagascar Hissing Cockroach
www.marylandzoo.org/animal/madagascar-hissing-cockroach/
Learn more about how hissing cockroaches live in the wild.

National Geographic Kids: Hissing Cockroaches
kids.nationalgeographic.com/animals/invertebrates/facts/hissing-cockroach
Check out photographs and videos with more facts about hissing cockroaches.

GLOSSARY

abdomen: The part of an insect's body that contains the organs to break down food.

communicate: To share thoughts or feelings by sound, movement, or writing.

ecosystem: A natural community of life that includes living and nonliving features.

hatch: To break open or come out of.

horn: A hard, pointed growth on an animal's head.

tank: A large container used to keep animals in as pets.

territory: An area of land that an animal considers to be its own and will fight to defend.

thorax: The middle part of an insect's body. The wings and legs connect to it.

INDEX